STRANGE SIGHTS IN THE WHITE HOUSE

and Other Hauntings in Washington, D.C.

by Megan Cooley Peterson

CAPSTONE PRESS

a capstone imprint

Capstone Captivate is published by Capstone Press, an imprint of Capstone.
1710 Roe Crest Drive
North Mankato, Minnesota 56003
www.capstonepub.com

Library of Congress Cataloging-in-Publication Data is available on the Library of Congress website.
ISBN: 978-1-4966-8373-1 (library binding)
ISBN: 978-1-4966-8424-0 (eBook PDF)

Summary: As the First Family sleeps, something spooky goes bump in the night. History knows the White House as the symbol of the American presidency. Could it also be America's most haunted house? Learn more about the White House's most talked-about ghosts and about other paranormal activity running wild in the nation's capital. Between these pages, readers will find just the right amount of scariness for a cold, dark night.

Image Credits
Alamy: Eric Nathan, middle 28, Historic Collection, tope left 29; iStockphoto: Georgethefourth, 17, GlobalP, 8; Library of Congress: Prints and Photographs Division Washington, D.C., 10 top 11, bottom 11, 12, 13; Newscom: Album, 22, Barbara Kinney/SIPA, top 15, Roger L. Wollenberg, 27; Pixabay: dannysantos, (wood) design element, geralt, (paper) design element; Shutterstock: Andrey_Popov, 25, Colin Dewar, 6, DC Studio, bottom 15, Everett Historical, top 9, 18, 24, John P Wainwright, bottom 9, Kristina Kokhanova, top 19, MIGUEL G. SAAVEDRA, 20, Orhan Cam, bottom left Cover, 16, Philip Rozenski, 23, Pierdelune, top Cover, Sean Pavone, 5, 21, Tish11, (map) 28-29, Vasiliy Koval, bottom 19, Victorian Traditions, 4; Wikimedia: Library of Congress, bottom right Cover

Editorial Credits
Editor: Renae Gilles; Designer: Sara Radka; Media Researcher: Morgan Walters; Production Specialist: Katy LaVigne

Quote Sources
p.10, "The White House's best ghost stories." National Constitution Center, Oct. 31, 2016; p.14, "Ghosts in the White House." History, Aug. 12, 2019; p.18, "John Quincy Adams." The National Children's Book and Literacy Alliance, 2020; p.26, "45% of Americans believe that ghosts and demons exist." YouGov.com, Oct. 21, 2019.

All internet sites appearing in back matter were available and accurate when this book was sent to press.

Printed and bound in the USA.
PA117

TABLE OF CONTENTS

Words in **bold** are in the glossary.

A HAUNTED CAPITAL

Washington, D.C., is the capital of the United States. Founded in 1790, it is home to the White House, the Capitol Building, and the Library of Congress. Millions of people visit the city each year. They tour government buildings and other famous **monuments**.

Washington, D.C., might also be home to something you won't hear about on most tours—ghosts! Many important people have lived and died in this city. For years, tales of haunted libraries and ghostly presidents have spread throughout the city. Are these tales true? No one knows for sure, but you can learn about the stories and decide for yourself!

FREAKY FACT

Washington, D.C., was named for President George Washington. But he never lived there. Washington died before the White House was completed.

A few of the 20 million annual visitors to the Lincoln Memorial Reflecting Pool and Washington Monument leave with stories of ghostly experiences.

CHAPTER 1

GHOSTS IN THE WHITE HOUSE

Visitors, staff members, presidents, and first ladies have all reported encounters with ghosts at the White House.

The president of the United States lives and works at the White House. Construction began in 1792 and was finished 8 years later. The White House has 132 rooms, 35 bathrooms, and 8 staircases. Some say it has ghosts too!

THE GHOST OF ANDREW JACKSON

Andrew Jackson served as president from 1829 to 1837. After a long illness, he died in 1845. His ghost is said to haunt his former residence. Since the 1860s, staff and visitors have reported Jackson's ghost in the Queen's Bedroom. They say his ghost lies in bed, laughing. Former first lady Mary Todd Lincoln said Jackson's ghost would stomp around the White House. When he was alive, Jackson was known for his bad temper.

TIMELINE OF PRESIDENTS AND FIRST LADIES WITH REPORTED GHOSTS

1789–1797: President George Washington and first lady Martha Washington

1797–1801: President John Adams and first lady Abigail Adams

1809–1817: President James Madison and first lady Dolley Madison

1829–1837: President Andrew Jackson and first lady Emily Donelson. (Donelson became first lady after her aunt and Jackson's wife Rachel died.)

1861–1865: President Abraham Lincoln and first lady Mary Todd Lincoln

1923–1929: President Calvin Coolidge and first lady Grace Coolidge

LINCOLN'S GHOST

President Abraham Lincoln's ghost is one of the most commonly reported **spirits** in the White House. Lincoln took office in 1861. He was killed in 1865. Some say his restless spirit still roams the house.

First lady Grace Coolidge once saw a ghostly figure in the Lincoln Bedroom. Lincoln used this room as an office when he lived there. Coolidge said Lincoln's ghost stood by the window. The window faced a **Civil War** (1861–1865) battlefield near the Potomac River. She thought he was looking at the battlefield.

FREAKY FACT

One of President Ronald Reagan's dogs was a Cavalier King Charles Spaniel. It refused to enter the Lincoln Bedroom. Some people believe it could sense the presence of ghosts!

A few weeks before he was killed, Abraham Lincoln had a dream about his own death.

Many world leaders say they've seen Lincoln's ghost at the White House. One of the most famous sightings took place in 1940. British Prime Minister Winston Churchill was staying in the White House. After taking a bath, he found that his bedroom wasn't empty. The ghost of Abraham Lincoln stood in the room. Churchill said, "Good evening, Mr. President. You seem to have me at a disadvantage." Then Lincoln's ghost disappeared.

In 1942, Queen Wilhelmina of the Netherlands stayed at the White House. Around midnight, someone knocked at her bedroom door. She found an unexpected visitor on the other side—Lincoln's ghost! The queen fainted.

Winston Churchill

The White House holds many antiques and pieces of historical furniture.

Mary Todd Lincoln

WHITE HOUSE SÉANCES

In 1862, 11-year-old Willie Lincoln died at the White House. He was the president's youngest son. Later, Mary Todd Lincoln held **séances** in the Red Room. During a séance, people try to speak with ghosts. These séances helped Mary deal with the death of her son. The Lincolns later said Willie's ghost visited them at the White House.

GHOSTLY FIRST LADIES

Former presidents aren't the only ghosts said to appear at the White House. The ghost of first lady Abigail Adams is said to haunt the East Room. Adams used this room to hang sheets after washing them. She died in 1818. People say her ghost remains, still folding sheets. Staff members have even reported smelling clean laundry in that room.

The large open space of the East Room is used for concerts, dances, and other large gatherings.

No one has tried to dig up the Rose Garden since the sighting of Dolley Madison's ghost more than 100 years ago.

The Rose Garden is a famous garden at the White House. First lady Ellen Wilson designed it in 1913. She died the following year. President Woodrow Wilson remarried in 1915. According to stories, his new wife, Edith, wanted to change the Rose Garden. But the ghost of first lady Dolley Madison scared workers away. Madison was first lady from 1809 to 1817. She was known for wearing fancy **turbans** on her head. Workers recognized her ghostly turban as she walked around the garden. They decided to leave the garden alone.

OTHER WHITE HOUSE GHOSTS

In 1790, the U.S. government created the city of Washington, D.C. But it first had to buy the land from private landowners. David Burns sold some of his farm to the government. Most of the city was built on his land, including the White House. But according to **legend**, he wasn't happy with the sale price. Burns's ghost has been seen in the Yellow Oval Room. His ghost reportedly told a staff member, "I'm Mr. Burns." Was his ghost still upset over the sale?

A ghostly boy was said to haunt the White House in 1911. Many workers said they saw the ghost of a young teenage boy. Sometimes, the ghost would touch their shoulders. No one knew who the ghost was or what it wanted. President William Taft threatened to fire anyone who discussed the ghost. It hasn't been reported since.

Presidents receive important guests in the Yellow Oval Room. The ghosts of Abraham Lincoln and Thomas Jefferson have also been seen there.

A GHOSTLY MUSICIAN?

In the early 2000s, first daughters Jenna and Barbara Bush were asleep one night. Suddenly, 1920s piano music mysteriously came through the fireplace in their bedroom. The following week, opera music drifted from the fireplace. The girls believed it was a ghost making the music.

CHAPTER 2

THE CAPITOL BUILDING

The Capitol Building is one of the most famous buildings on Earth. It houses the Senate and the House of Representatives. Construction began in 1793. President George Washington even laid one of its first stones. Some say it's the most haunted place in Washington, D.C.

At least 15 different ghosts have been recorded in the Capitol Building since the late 1800s.

CIVIL WAR GHOSTS

The Civil War (1861–1865) almost broke the United States apart. The Union wanted to keep the country together. The Confederates wanted to start their own nation. The Union won, and the country remained united. During the war, part of the Capitol was used as a hospital. Wounded Union soldiers were brought to Statuary Hall. At least 1,000 cots were placed in the room. Some say at least one soldier never left. His ghostly shadow has been seen moving around the room.

After the war, Union General John Logan served as a senator. He died in 1886. Some say his ghost returns to the old Military Affairs Committee room in the Capitol. It was once used by the Military Affairs Committee. Blue light surrounds Logan's ghost.

Ghost experts claim that the spirits of people who die suddenly, such as some soldiers, are often confused and refuse to move on.

A FALLEN PRESIDENT

In 1848, former President John Quincy Adams was on the House floor. There was a vote on whether to pass a new law. Adams loudly voted, "No!" Then he collapsed. Adams was moved into a side room. He fell into a coma and died there. Late at night, some Capitol staff members have reported hearing a ghostly voice shouting, "No!"

John Quincy Adams reportedly did not enjoy his time as president, calling it "The four most miserable years of my life."

THE DEMON CAT

In the 1800s, a night guard was patrolling the Capitol. Suddenly, a black cat walked toward him. As the cat came closer, it grew larger. Soon, it was as big as a tiger! The cat pounced on the guard. Then it vanished.

Nicknamed the "demon cat," it's been spotted in the Capitol ever since. Some say there is proof the ghost is real. In 1898, some of the stone floor in the small Senate rotunda was damaged. Workers replaced the stone with concrete. The concrete has several cat prints. Many people say the demon cat left those prints.

CHAPTER 3

THE LIBRARY OF CONGRESS

The Library of Congress is the largest library in the United States. Built in 1897, it houses more than 39 million books. Some say ghosts are hidden among the shelves.

A FRIENDLY GHOST

The Library of Congress fills three buildings in Washington, D.C. It's easy to get lost. People lost in the Thomas Jefferson Building may get some otherworldly help. A ghostly police officer is said to haunt this building. Witnesses say he helps people who are lost. The ghost even has friendly conversations with them. Many people believe he died in the library.

FREAKY FACT

The 1984 movie *Ghostbusters* is preserved at the Library of Congress. As of 2020, 775 movies have been given that honor. The library chooses movies that are important to American **culture**.

The Library of Congress has 838 miles (1,349 kilometers) of bookshelves.

STILL WORKING

The basement of the Jefferson Building might also be haunted. According to stories, a man worked in the basement stamping books. He died around 1900, shortly after the library was built. Today, workers report seeing his ghost quietly stamping books.

CHAPTER 4

SPIRITS OF THE SMITHSONIAN

A large stone castle on the National Mall is said to be haunted. Called the Smithsonian Castle, it was built in 1847. English scientist James Smithson died in 1829. He left his money to the U.S. government. Smithson wanted the government to start a research **institute** in his name. Congress created the Smithsonian Institution in 1846. The castle is the original building. Today, the Smithsonian includes several museums.

James Smithson left $500,000 to the U.S. government. Today, that would be worth more than $12 million.

The Smithsonian Castle was troubled from the start. To lower costs, builders used wood beams instead of iron. The wood was not as strong. By February 1850, the floor began to sink. Workers had to replace the beams. In March, a worker slipped off some **scaffolding** while making repairs and died.

The sad events didn't end. Many people who lived in the castle died there. Joseph Henry worked as the Smithsonian's secretary. He lived in the castle with his family. In 1862, his son came home ill. He died in the building. In 1876, scientist Fielding Meek also died in the castle. Joseph Henry later died there himself in 1878.

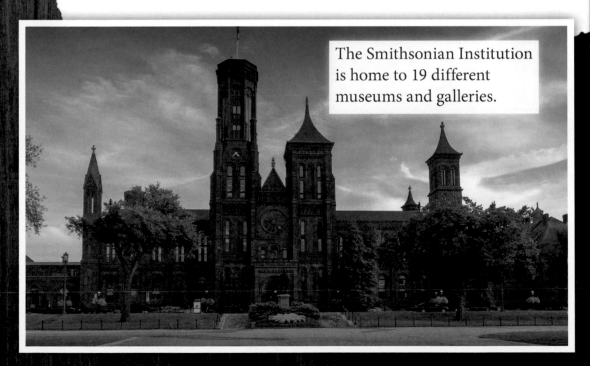

The Smithsonian Institution is home to 19 different museums and galleries.

As early as 1900, people began reporting strange sounds and sights at the castle. They heard ghostly voices and footsteps when no one else was around. Night guards even came face-to-face with Joseph Henry's ghost.

In 1904, James Smithson's remains were placed in a **crypt** inside the building. Workers made repairs to the crypt in 1974. They removed Smithson's coffin. Scientists studied his skeleton. After two days, his remains were placed back inside his coffin.

Smithson's ghost has been seen around the castle ever since. Doors open and close by themselves. Library books fly off the shelves. Ghostly voices ring through the building. Some say Smithson is angry his remains were disturbed.

FREAKY FACT

James Smithson died in Italy. In 1904, inventor Alexander Graham Bell had Smithson's remains brought to the United States.

Alexander Graham Bell

Night guards need to investigate reports of strange happenings in buildings.

CHAPTER 5

OLD STONE HOUSE

Old Stone House is the oldest standing building in Washington, D.C. It was built in the mid-1760s. Later, it housed a clock shop and a car dealership. Today, it's a museum.

As many as 11 ghosts are said to haunt the building. A woman in an old-fashioned dress floats near the fireplace. Another ghostly woman in a fancy dress visits the kitchen. She has also been seen on the staircase. A ghostly man with long blond hair stares out a front window. The ghosts at Old Stone House seem friendly, except for a ghost named George. George haunts the third floor. His ghost reportedly shoves and chokes people.

DO YOU BELIEVE IN GHOSTS?

36% of Americans have felt the presence of a ghost.

43% of Americans believe ghosts can haunt a place or people.

45% of Americans believe ghosts and demons are real.

Visitors report a feeling of being unwelcome at the Old Stone House.

In 2018, a man and his wife visited Old Stone House at night. They took photos and recorded audio. While on the first floor, the man thought he saw something move. When they listened to the audio, they heard something strange. A mysterious voice on the audio grunted "No." Could it have been one of the ghosts?

Haunted Places of
WASHINGTON, D.C.

1. **The Capitol Building**

2. **The White House**

3. **Old Stone House**

4. **Library of Congress**

5. **Smithsonian Castle**

Hay-Adams Hotel

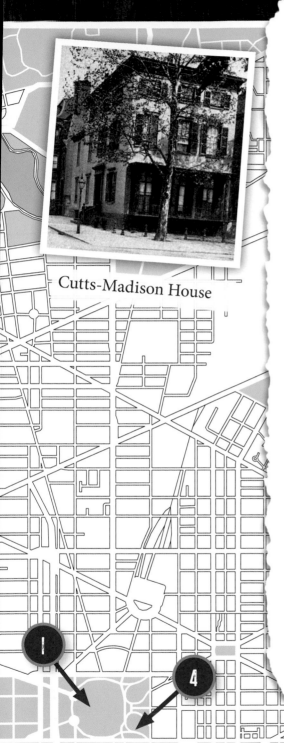

Cutts-Madison House

6. **Octagon House**

   Colonel John Tayloe built this mansion from 1798 to 1800. The ghosts of his two daughters are said to haunt the house.

7. **Cutts-Madison House**

   Dolley Madison lived at this house for the last few years of her life. Her ghost has been seen on the front porch.

8. **The Hay-Adams Hotel**

   Built in 1927, this hotel is home to a ghostly woman named Marian Hooper Adams. She died on the land in 1885. Guests have reported a ghostly woman crying. Radios turn off and on by themselves.

GLOSSARY

Civil War (SIV-il WOR)—the battle between states in the North and South that led to the end of slavery in the United States

crypt (KRIPT)—a chamber used as a grave

culture (KUHL-chuhr)—a people's way of life, ideas, customs, and traditions

institute (IN-stuh-toot)—a group that is set up to protect animals, people, and other causes

legend (LEJ-uhnd)—a story handed down from earlier times; legends are often based on fact, but they are not entirely true

monument (MON-yuh-muhnt)—a statue or building that is meant to remind people of an event or a person

scaffolding (SKAF-ol-ding)—temporary framework or set of platforms used to support workers and materials

séance (SAY-ahnss)—a meeting at which people try to make contact with the dead

spirit (SPIHR-it)—the soul or invisible part of a person that is believed to control thoughts and feelings; some people believe the spirit leaves the body after death

turban (TUR-bin)—a headdress made by winding a long cloth around the head

READ MORE

Brinker, Spencer. *Wretched Washington.* New York: Bearport Publishing Company, Inc., 2019.

Gagne, Tammy. *Ghosts of the White House.* North Mankato: MN: Capstone Press, 2018.

Morrison, Marie. *The White House Is Haunted!* New York: PowerKids Press, 2020.

INTERNET SITES

Ghosts in the White House
https://www.history.com/topics/halloween/ghosts-in-the-white-house

Haunted Halls of Congress: 5 Creepy Capitol Legends
https://www.aoc.gov/blog/haunted-halls-congress-5-creepy-capitol-legends

White House Ghost Stories
https://www.whitehousehistory.org/press-room/press-fact-sheets/white-house-ghost-stories

White House Virtual Tour
https://artsandculture.google.com/partner/the-white-house

INDEX